Soul Rich

For the Woman Coming Home to Herself and Her Money

BY
KALEE BOISVERT

Soul Rich: For the Woman Coming Home to Herself and Her Money
Copyright © 2025 by Kalee Boisvert
All rights reserved.

No part of this book may be reproduced, stored in a retrieval system, or transmitted in any form or by any means—electronic, mechanical, photocopying, recording, or otherwise—without the prior written permission of the publisher, except in the case of brief quotations embodied in critical articles or reviews.

This is a work of nonfiction. The content is based on personal experience and reflection. While the author has made every effort to ensure the accuracy and completeness of the information contained herein, this book is not intended to serve as financial, legal, or medical advice. Readers are encouraged to consult with appropriate professionals for personalized guidance.

First edition, 2025

Contents

Introduction	1
Chapter 1: She Thought Money Was the Problem	3
Chapter 2: She Didn't Know How to Receive	9
Chapter 3: She Had Enough But Still Didn't Feel Safe	15
Chapter 4: When Money Felt Like Proof	19
Chapter 5: She Thought She Had to Do It All Herself	23
Chapter 6: The Shame She Didn't Name	27
Chapter 7: She Didn't Trust Herself Yet	31
Chapter 8: She Was Learning to Let It Feel Good	35
Chapter 9: She Reclaimed Her Wanting	39
Chapter 10: When Gratitude Becomes a Cage	43
Chapter 11: She Let It Be Easy	49
Chapter 12: She Was Allowed to Rest	55
Chapter 13: She Stopped Comparing	59
Chapter 14: She Stopped Rushing	63
Chapter 15: She No Longer Tied Her Worth to the Numbers	67
Chapter 16: She Learned to Forgive Her Past Self	73

Chapter 17: She Saw the Pattern, and This Time She Chose Differently … 77

Chapter 18: She Stopped Feeling Ashamed of What She Didn't Know … 83

Chapter 19: She Redefined What It Meant to Be "Good with Money" … 87

Chapter 20: She Realized She Wasn't Starting From Scratch … 91

Chapter 21: She Became the Source … 95

Chapter 22: She Didn't Have to Hustle to Be Worthy … 99

Chapter 23: She Didn't Wait to Feel Ready … 103

Chapter 24: She Faced the Numbers—And Didn't Fall Apart … 107

Chapter 25: She Asked for What She Needed—Even When Her Voice Shook … 111

Chapter 26: She Released the Pressure to Always Be Doing More … 115

Chapter 27: She Trusted Her Inner Yes-Even If It Didn't Make Sense on Paper … 119

Chapter 28: She Stopped Chasing More Just to Feel Enough … 123

Chapter 29: She Realized It Wasn't Just About the Money-It Was About Her Freedom … 127

Chapter 30: A Life That Holds All of You … 131

Acknowledgments … 135

Introduction

This book isn't about getting rich fast.
It's about coming home.
To the part of you that already is—and always has been—rich.

Rich in wisdom.
Rich in resilience.
Rich in self-worth, even when it felt hard to find.

For so many women, money has been a source of stress, shame, or silence.
We've been taught to stay small.
To be grateful—but not ask for too much.
To let someone else handle the numbers.
To disconnect from our own value.

But that story is no longer yours to carry.

You don't have to do it the way they did.
You don't have to hustle to prove your worth.
You don't have to wait until you're debt-free, confident, or "good with money" to begin.

You get to start from right here.
With honesty.
With softness.
With curiosity.

Soul Rich is not a step-by-step formula.
It's a remembering.

Of who you are.
Of what matters.
Of how deeply worthy you've always been.

The book unfolds in 30 short chapters that blend money truths with soul truths.
Each one includes a **Money Wisdom** reflection and a **Soul Bank Practice**—gentle steps to help you build a life that reflects your values, your clarity, and your wholeness.

Whether you're healing from burnout, rewriting old money stories,
or simply ready to build wealth that feels good on the inside too—
this book is here to walk with you.

Not to fix you.
Because I don't believe you were ever broken.

This has existed inside you all along.

And I wrote this to walk beside you as you remember that truth:

You were never a lost cause.
You are not "bad with money."
You are worthy of ease and joy.
And you are allowed to become soul rich.

Chapter One
She Thought Money Was the Problem

She blamed money for the problem.
It never seemed to be on her side.
There was never quite enough.
And when it did show up, it never stayed—
leaving just as quickly as it came.

The number on the screen never settled the tightness in her chest.
Some days, debt loomed like a shadow.
And peace felt like something she could only earn
once every dollar was paid off.

The impulse to check, recheck, and track every cent
became a quiet obsession.
Fear was always just a breath away.
And she spiraled through every version of not enough:
If I could just make a little more…
If I could just get ahead…
Then maybe I could finally exhale.

But no matter what she earned,
the unease stayed.

Because the real problem wasn't the numbers.
What she feared wasn't money itself.
It was the weight she had given it.
The story behind the balance.
The meaning money had taken on in her life—over years, over decades.

It was her relationship with it.
The stories she had absorbed from everyone but herself.
The nervous system that had learned to brace, to grip, to go without.
The scarcity she inherited and carried.

It lived beneath the surface—
always present, always preparing for the worst with each purchase she made.

It echoed in childhood,
when money was limited and spoken about in low tones.
It showed up at school,
where being "good" meant collecting gold stars.
It crept into work,
where hard work became a badge.
And even into motherhood,
where putting herself last was called love.

So, she kept chasing safety—
through money,
through working hard,
through doing more than she had to,
for longer than she wanted to.

Because some part of her still believed that in the doing, she would finally prove her worth.

It took time to see it clearly.
What had felt like a money issue
was actually a self-worth issue.
A safety issue.
A fear-of-not-enough issue.

And once she saw it, something softened.
Not all at once—
but just enough.

A small crack.
A shift.
The kind of breaking that lets healing in.

Money Wisdom

Money isn't the enemy.
And it's not the answer to everything either.

It's a mirror.

It reflects how safe you feel,
how much you trust,
and where you may have been selling yourself short.

Most of us weren't taught to feel at ease with money.
We were taught to control it, fear it,
or prove our value through it.

But here's the truth:
Your worth was never meant to be measured by what you earn.
Safety doesn't live in a spreadsheet.
And peace isn't something you have to earn by doing more.

What if money could feel different?
Not because your income suddenly skyrockets—

but because you begin to shift how you *see* it.
How you *relate* to it.

Because you stay with yourself when the fear rises.
You choose pause instead of panic.
You try a new story—one that actually fits who you are.

You are not hopeless.
You are not behind.
This isn't a race.

You are becoming more aware.
And awareness is where everything begins to change.

Your relationship with money gets to feel safer.
Softer.
Steadier.

Not someday.
Starting now.

Soul Bank Practice: Rewriting the Root

Step 1: Feel the Pattern
When you think about money, where do you feel it in your body?
Tight chest? Spinning head? Clenched stomach?
Pause. Place your hand there.
Breathe into that space.
No fixing. No rushing. Just noticing.

Step 2: Name the Story
What story does your brain tell you about money?
Write it down—honestly and without judgment.

Examples:
- "It's always about to run out."
- "I'll never get ahead."
- "I have to do it all alone."
- "If I don't control it, everything will fall apart."

Step 3: Trace the Inheritance
Where do you think that story came from?
Was it something you saw growing up?
Was it taught to you—directly or indirectly?
Whose fear might you still be carrying?

Step 4: Choose the Rewrite
Ask yourself gently:
What's the deeper truth I'm ready to believe about money now?
Let it rise.
Write it down. Say it out loud.

This is your new deposit into your Soul Bank—
a currency that grows in peace, not pressure.

Chapter Two
She Didn't Know How to Receive

She thought the hardest part would be making money.
But it turned out that receiving it was even harder.

Not the act of it landing in her hands.
She knew how to open a bank account, accept an e-transfer, cash a check.
That wasn't the issue.

The issue was what happened inside her
when something good actually came in.

A compliment.
An unexpected refund.
Someone offering to pay.
A little extra.
More ease than she planned for.

Whenever she was given something,
her body tensed.
Her voice deflected.

She Didn't Know How to Receive

She'd say things like:
"You didn't have to."
"Next one's on me."
"Oh, this old thing?"
"No no, I've got it."

It wasn't just being polite.
It was discomfort.

Letting goodness in felt unfamiliar.
Wobbly.
Like if she allowed too much ease,
she might owe something in return.
Or be seen as selfish.
Or lose control.

And underneath all of it
was the quiet belief that she wasn't allowed to receive
unless she had fully earned it.

So even when money came,
she found subtle ways to push it away.
Not always on purpose.

Overspending.
Overgiving.
Overjustifying.

Because it didn't feel safe to simply have.
To hold.
To trust that she didn't have to trade herself
to be taken care of.

What she was really learning
was that she had always been deserving.

Money Wisdom

Receiving isn't a reward for being good.
It's balance.
It's the other side of giving.

But it's the side most of us were never really taught.

We learned how to give.
To stretch.
To take care of others.
To say "It's fine" when it wasn't.

But we weren't taught how to stay open
when something nourishing came toward us.
How to believe in possibilities beyond what we expected.

So we brace.
We deflect.
We grip the illusion of control
because surrender feels too soft, too risky, too good to be true.

But here's the truth:
If you can't receive money without guilt,
you'll keep pushing it away
even if you don't mean to.

And no amount of budgeting, earning, or planning
can override what your nervous system is quietly rejecting.

Receiving is the muscle.
Money is the invitation.

And every time you choose to allow,
to stay open,
to breathe through the discomfort of ease,
you're building something new.

A foundation where you don't have to give your all just to feel worthy.

A life where you trust that what's meant for you will arrive and you'll know how to let it in.

Soul Bank Practice: Softening Into Enough

Step 1: Notice the Discomfort
Think of the last time someone gave you something—
a gift, a compliment, money, or help.
What was your first instinct?
Did you fully receive it, or did you try to brush it off or downplay it?

Step 2: Let Yourself Replay It
Close your eyes and bring that moment back to mind.
But this time, stay open.
Let the compliment land.
Let the support in.
Breathe into the part of you that wanted to deflect.
You don't have to earn it. You're allowed to receive.

Step 3: Rewrite the Script
Write down a new response you could try next time.
Something simple, honest, and grounded.
Examples:
"Thank you. That means a lot."
"I receive that."
Or just... "Yes."

Step 4: Practice in Small Ways
Today, let yourself receive one small thing without apology.
A kind word. A helpful gesture. A compliment. A breath.
Let it in without shrinking or explaining.
This is a deposit into your Soul Bank.
One that doesn't require proof—only presence and allowing.

Chapter Three
She Had Enough But Still Didn't Feel Safe

For years, she thought the answer was more money.
She was sure that once she had it
really had it, not just scraping by
the problems would be solved.
That she would feel settled.
And safe.

She imagined checking her bank account and breathing easy.
Sleeping through the night without mentally shuffling credit card balances or unexpected bills.
She imagined the ease, what it would be like to not carry that weight anymore.

And then one day, after all her diligent saving and hard work, she got there.
Maybe not rich, but stable.
A reliable income.
A fully funded emergency account.
Some breathing room.

The kind of life she used to dream about
when she was barely getting out of the red.

But the strangest thing happened.
She didn't become the image of ease and calm.
Her body didn't relax.
She still tensed at the sight of a bill in the mail pile.
Still flinched at the idea of spending on something non-essential.
Still checked her accounts more often than she liked
just to make sure it was really okay.
That it hadn't vanished
or been wiped out by some bank error or fraud.

And it was okay.
But she wasn't.

Because money wasn't the real source of her fear.
The patterns had taken root long before the pay raises.
The part of her that had learned to anticipate lack,
plan for the worst,
expect problems,
and just get by to survive
that part hadn't gotten the update.

Her nervous system was still stuck in an old loop.
Even when the numbers finally said, "You're safe,"
her body whispered, "Don't trust it."

She thought money was the solution.
But what she really needed was healing.
To feel safe in herself
not just in her bank account.

And that kind of safety?
It wasn't something she could buy.

It was something she had to acknowledge and allow.
Gently.
Slowly.
Moment by moment.

Money Wisdom

Safety doesn't live in a certain number on a screen.
It arrives when your body no longer feels like it's under threat.

Money can support that healing,
but it's not a switch you flip.

Feeling secure comes from trust.
Trust in your ability to respond to life.
Trust in your relationship with yourself.
Trust in the quiet knowing that you are already held.

If you've reached financial stability and still feel anxious,
it doesn't mean you need a bigger number.
It means you're human.

There is nothing wrong with you.
You're just untangling fear from truth.
Scarcity from safety.
Control from peace.

And the more you choose pause over panic,
compassion over control,
peace over perfection—
the safer you'll feel.

Soul Bank Practice: Rebuilding Safety

Step 1: Name the Old Script

Finish the sentence:
"I thought once I had _____, I would feel safe."

Step 2: Listen to Your Body

When you look at your finances right now, does your body agree that you're safe?
Where is there tension, gripping, or resistance?

Step 3: Remind Yourself What's True Now

Write down three things that are different now from your past.
Examples:
I know how to ask for help.
I've made it through hard things before.

Step 4: Define Safety on Your Terms

What does true safety mean to you?
Not what the world told you.
Not what the spreadsheet says.
What does your version of safety feel like?

Say This Out Loud:
"Safety is not from a number.
It's something I can rebuild from within."

Chapter Four
When Money Felt Like Proof

She didn't realize how deeply she was using money to prove something.
Not in a flashy pink Lamborghini way.
She wasn't chasing status symbols.

She just wanted to be okay.
To be taken seriously.
To be enough.

So when the raise came, she felt valuable.
When the numbers looked strong, she felt confident.
When the client said yes, she felt seen.

But when things slowed down—
when income dipped,
when something went wrong—
she started to sink.

Her worth dropped with her earnings.
Her mood tanked with her bank account.

She didn't just feel disappointed.
She felt like a failure.

Because somewhere along the way,
money had become proof that she mattered.
That she was doing life right.
That she was responsible.
That she was allowed to take up space.
The symbol of success.

And without it, she felt like she was failing.

She didn't know how to feel valuable
without having numbers to back it up.
She didn't know how to feel proud of herself
unless she could point to something she'd done, created, or accomplished.

She didn't know how to rest
without guilt tagging along beside her—
so she didn't.

Because money wasn't just a tool.
It was a trophy.

And for a long time, it reflected back a version of her
that had to keep performing
just to feel lovable.

Money Wisdom

You likely learned early on that you had to prove your worth through doing—
so it makes sense that money got wrapped up in that too.

Money became the measure of success.
Numbers became how you tracked progress.
How you proved you weren't lazy.
How you convinced yourself you weren't behind.

But your worth isn't earned by the number of zeros behind your balance.
And your value doesn't rise and fall with your income.

That's a system you absorbed—probably young.
A system that taught you:
success equals safety,
and safety equals love.

But that system is flawed.

You don't have to earn your way into being okay.
And love isn't conditional.

Money can be a resource, not a scoreboard.
A support, not a verdict.
A reflection of how you care for yourself—
not how hard you push yourself.

Your softness doesn't make you weak.
Your rest doesn't make you less.
Your presence—not your performance—
is what truly holds power.

You are not the number.
You never were.

Soul Bank Practice: Proof-Free Value

Step 1: Find the Pattern
When do you most feel like your worth is tied to money?
After a big win?
A financial mistake?
A conversation with someone?

Step 2: Detach the Outcome
Write a short list of what you're proud of
that has nothing to do with results, numbers, or output.
Think: effort, integrity, kindness, courage.

Step 3: Challenge the Scoreboard
Finish this sentence:
Even if I make no more money this month, I am still…
Examples: worthy, powerful, enough, supported.

Step 4: Build a New Proof
Every time you catch yourself tying your worth to money, pause.
Take a breath.
Then say—out loud or silently:
"My worth is already decided. I'm just remembering it now."

You're not here to prove yourself.
You're here to live from who you already are.
That's your wealth.
That's the real proof.

Chapter Five
She Thought She Had to Do It All Herself

Somewhere along the way,
she decided it was safer not to need anyone.

Maybe it came from watching her mom hold it all together without much help.
Maybe it was the sting of being let down one too many times.
Maybe it was the way people praised her for being independent.
Or maybe it was just the quiet message she picked up over time—strong women do it all.

So she became the one who could be counted on.
The one who made the plans, paid the bills, sent the thank-you cards, kept it all running.
The one who remembered the things no one else seemed to notice.
The one who didn't ask for much, but gave a lot.

Even when she was tired.
Even when she didn't have the capacity.
Even when she wished someone would step in and say,
"I've got you. You can rest now."

But she didn't ask.
Because what if needing help made her weak?
What if dropping the ball meant she wasn't capable after all?

So she kept holding it all.
The work.
The groceries.
The appointments.
The invisible labor.
The emotional load.
The mental math of how long the money would stretch.

Even when she had support around her.
Even when she wasn't technically doing life alone.
She still felt like she had to be the one holding it all together.

Because somewhere deep inside,
she believed she was supposed to.
That asking for help made her less.
That real strength meant not needing anyone.

It made her reliable.
It made her proud sometimes.
But it also made her lonely.

And eventually, she saw it.

Doing it all wasn't a badge of honor.
It was a survival strategy.
A way to feel safe.
A way to stay in control.

But she didn't have to live like that anymore.
Not just surviving.
Not just holding it all.

She could be supported too.
She could let herself be held.

And that didn't make her weak.
It made her free.

Money Wisdom

You weren't meant to carry it all.
And doing everything yourself isn't the only way to prove you're strong.

Financial independence is powerful.
But it doesn't mean never needing anyone.
It doesn't mean gritting your teeth through the burnout.
It doesn't mean earning your way into rest.

Receiving is not weakness.
Collaboration is not failure.
Support is not dependency.

You're allowed to take a breath.
To share the load.
To let money support you.
To let people support you.

You are not less for needing help.
You are not more for going it alone.
You're just human.
And worthy of ease.

You are allowed to be held.
And that might be the richest soul feeling of all.

Soul Bank Practice: Unlearning the Lone-Wolf Habit

Step 1: Spot the Pattern
Where in your life are you still carrying more than you need to?
What are you holding that could be shared, delegated, or released?

Step 2: Unpack the Belief
What does your inner voice say when you think about asking for help?
Examples:
They'll think I can't handle it.
No one will do it right.
It's just easier to do it myself.

Step 3: Remember the Truth
What would it feel like to trust someone else with part of the weight?
What would it feel like to receive support—
not because you earned it,
but simply because you're worthy of it?

Step 4: Take a Micro-Action
Ask for help today.
Let someone step in.
Receive without guilt.
Say yes when ease knocks.

This is how you begin to rewrite the story.
Not as the woman who always held it all together,
but as the one who finally let herself be held.

Chapter Six
The Shame She Didn't Name

It didn't scream.
It didn't shout.
It just sat quietly in the background.
That low hum of not-enough.

Not responsible enough.
Not money-smart enough.
Not where she thought she *should* be by now.

It showed up when she thought about the credit card she hadn't paid off.
When she compared herself to friends who seemed to have it all together.
When she remembered a past mistake and still felt the flush of regret.

Sometimes it looked like guilt.
Sometimes like embarrassment.
But underneath, it was shame.

The kind that sticks.

It didn't matter that she'd made progress.
That she was learning.
That she was showing up with more awareness than ever before.

Shame didn't care.
It had already decided she was behind.
Already whispered that she wasn't good with money.

It told her not to talk about it.
Not to ask questions.
Not to admit she didn't have it all figured out—
because what would people think?
How would she look?

So she hid it.
Her doubts. Her past. Her fears.

Until one day, someone else said something honest.
They named their own struggle.
And instead of judgment, she felt... relief.

She realized something important:
Shame feeds on secrecy.
But the moment we speak it out loud
it starts to lose its grip.

Money Wisdom

Shame feels personal.
But a lot of the time it's cultural.

We live in a world that shames debt.
Shames desire.
Shames not knowing.

We're expected to manage money perfectly
without ever really being taught how.

Most of us didn't learn this in school.
We weren't given practice, support, or safe spaces to ask questions.

So we hide.
We blame ourselves for not knowing
what no one ever showed us.

But shame thrives in silence.
And the moment you say the thing out loud
to a friend, a partner, a coach, or even just in your journal
it starts to loosen.

Because you were never the only one.
And your money story, no matter how tangled or messy,
doesn't get to define your worth.

You're allowed to grow.
To change.
To let go of what was never yours to carry in the first place.

You don't have to keep apologizing for being human.
You just have to stay honest enough to heal.
And every single day is a chance to begin again.

Soul Bank Practice: Naming What Shame Hides

Step 1: Bring It Into the Light
What part of your money story do you feel ashamed about?
Write it down.
Even if it feels small. Even if it feels big.

Step 2: Get Curious
Where do you think that shame came from?
Was it modeled? Inherited? Absorbed from culture?

Step 3: Offer Compassion
If someone you loved was carrying that same shame, what would you say to them?

Step 4: Say This Out Loud
"This part of my story doesn't disqualify me.
It makes me real.
And I'm allowed to grow without shame trailing behind me."

Every time you speak shame into the open,
you reclaim a piece of your power.

And every time you meet yourself with compassion,
you make a new deposit into your Soul Bank.

You are not the shame.
You are the one brave enough to name it—and let it go.

Chapter Seven
She Didn't Trust Herself Yet

She never really felt like one of those people
The spreadsheet people
The savings-goal people
The ones who actually stuck to their budgets and had a plan for investing

She was the one who forgot due dates
Who bought the thing she didn't plan to buy
And felt guilty the second after
The one who checked her bank account like it might bite
Holding her breath before the number loaded

It wasn't that she didn't care about money
She cared a lot
So much it kept her up some nights

But somewhere along the way, she decided
I'm just not good with money
And she started saying it like it was a fact
Like her eye color or height
Something fixed
Unchangeable

She didn't realize how much that one sentence shaped everything
How it made her second-guess her own instincts
Made her hand over control, thinking she couldn't be trusted
Made her avoid the very things that actually needed her attention

She thought it was a flaw
But it wasn't
It was a story

A story built from past experiences
From what she saw growing up
From fear
From shame
From the belief that no one ever showed her a better way

No one had taught her how to trust herself with money
So she assumed she wasn't meant to

But what if she was wrong?

Money Wisdom

You don't have to be "good with money" in the way you might think.
You don't need a finance degree.
You don't need to love spreadsheets.
You don't have to understand every term or piece of jargon.

What you *do* need is the willingness to show up.
To look at your money with curiosity instead of fear.
To stay present instead of checking out.
To make choices that reflect what actually matters to *you*—
not just what's expected, or what everyone else is doing.

Being good with money isn't about doing it perfectly.
It's about being in relationship with it.
It's about presence.

It's not about never making mistakes.
It's about learning from them without beating yourself up.
It's about building self-trust, one small moment at a time.

Your brain might have picked up old scripts like:
I'm just bad with money.
I always mess this up.
I'm not smart enough for this.

But those stories aren't facts.
They're just habits of thought.
And you're allowed to rewrite them.

You're not behind.
You're not broken.
You're capable.
And you're allowed to believe in yourself now,
even before everything is "figured out."

Soul Bank Practice: Reclaiming Your Capability

Step 1: Name the old identity
Finish this sentence:
For as long as I can remember, I've believed I'm...
Bad with money. Not responsible.
Not disciplined. Not good enough.
Whatever comes up—just name it. No judgment.

Step 2: Ask where that story came from
Was it a moment? A pattern?
Someone else's voice you started to believe?
Get curious about it. You weren't born thinking this way—
it was learned. And what's learned can be unlearned.

Step 3: Name what you've done well
Even if they feel small.
Write down a few money moments you're proud of.
Times you showed up, paid attention, chose wisely.
Maybe you asked a hard question.
Said no when it mattered.
Opened a savings account.
These moments are proof.

Step 4: Say this out loud
I'm learning. I'm growing.
And I don't have to be perfect to be powerful.

You don't have to wait until you feel 100% ready.
You're allowed to begin from where you are—
imperfect, present, and more capable than you know.

Every time you show up with intention,
you make a deposit into your Soul Bank.
And confidence, like wealth, grows with care

Chapter Eight
She Was Learning to Let It Feel Good

The numbers were fine.
Actually, they were better than fine.
The bills were covered.
There was savings in place.
No immediate crisis.

And still...
she noticed how often she tensed up when checking her account.
How she couldn't buy something small without doing mental math.
How she waited for the other shoe to drop, even when things were calm.

It wasn't panic anymore.
It was something quieter.
A hum of unease she didn't know how to turn off.

She had already realized safety wasn't just a number.
But now she was learning what it meant to *feel* safe.
To let herself soften.
To let the stability be real.
To stop trying to "stay ahead" just in case.

There was still a part of her that believed peace had to be earned.
That ease was indulgent.
That joy needed justification.

But that part was learning something new:
she didn't need to be on high alert to be responsible.
She didn't need to keep hustling just to stay worthy.
She didn't have to hold her breath while life was good.

Because healing wasn't just surviving the hard seasons—
it was letting herself actually enjoy the good ones.
And that was a different kind of courage.
A different kind of wealth.

Money Wisdom

There's a difference between knowing you're safe—and letting yourself *feel* it.
You can have the emergency fund.
The stable income.
The cushion in your account.
And still live like the floor might fall out any second.

Because your nervous system doesn't heal just because your budget balances.
It heals when you let in softness.
When you pause and notice the absence of crisis—
and allow that absence to feel true.

You don't have to keep rehearsing for chaos.
You don't have to keep proving you're prepared.

Letting yourself feel peace isn't irresponsible.
It's the next step.
It's the work of integration.

It's how you let your body, your heart, and your soul catch up to the truth:
You are okay.
Right now, you are okay.
And you don't have to earn that feeling.
You just have to allow it.

Soul Bank Practice: Let It Feel Good

Step 1: Notice the Default
When things are going well, do you brace for something to go wrong?
Do you double-check your accounts, your inbox, your calendar—just in case?

Step 2: Pause and Name What's True Now
Take a breath.
Say it out loud:
"I am not in crisis. I am safe right now. My body can soften here."

Step 3: Welcome the Absence of Stress
Instead of waiting for the next problem, notice what *isn't* happening.
What does calm feel like in your body, even for a moment?

Step 4: Practice Letting It Be Enough
Do one small thing today without guilt or justification.
Buy the flowers. Rest for five minutes. Let someone help.
Let it feel good—on purpose.
Let that be your new normal.

Chapter Nine
She Reclaimed Her Wanting

She didn't even realize she was doing it.

At first, it just looked like being reasonable.
Choosing the cheaper version.
Saying, *"I don't really need that."*
Telling herself, *"I should just be grateful."*

And she was.
She really was grateful.
But over time, her wants got smaller.

Not because her soul wanted less—
but because the world had taught her she *should*.

She started explaining every purchase before anyone could ask.
It was on sale.
I've saved for years.
This is the first thing I've bought all year.

She didn't want to be selfish.
Didn't want to seem dramatic.
Didn't want to be labeled high maintenance.

So she shrank.
Quietly. Gradually.

She edited her desires into something more acceptable.
Toned down her vision.
Chose the safer route.

Because sometimes, it felt easier to shrink the want
than to feel the ache of not getting it.

She told herself she didn't really want that much.
That she was fine with less.
That she could get by.
That she shouldn't be so... *much*.

But the truth?
She *did* want more.

Not just more stuff—
More aliveness.
More joy.
More truth.
More *her*.

And eventually, she realized—
it was never about whether she *deserved* more.
It was about whether she was willing to *allow* it.

Money Wisdom

You might have learned to shape your wants
around what felt appropriate.

Not too expensive.
Not too indulgent.
Not too loud.

Maybe you were praised for being content with less.
Admired for your self-sacrifice.
Taught that wanting more meant being ungrateful.

But what if your desires aren't the problem?
What if they're actually a compass—
a signal from your soul
pointing you toward more truth, more expression, more of *you*?

Wanting something doesn't make you greedy.
It makes you honest.

Desire doesn't mean you don't appreciate what you have.
It means you're alive.

You're allowed to want what you want.
Not because you've earned it,
not because you've worked yourself to the edge—
but because you're finally ready to stop pretending you don't.

And that kind of honesty?
It's always worth listening to.

Soul Bank Practice: Letting Yourself Want

Step 1: Name What You've Shrunk
What have you talked yourself out of wanting?
Where have you told yourself, *That's too much. I shouldn't need that*?
Write it all down—no censoring, no judging.

Step 2: Listen for the Voices
What stories show up as you read your list?
Do you hear:
That's selfish.
You haven't earned it.
You're fine with less.
Those voices aren't your truth.
They're your training.

Step 3: Reclaim One Want
Choose one thing—big or small.
Let yourself say it, clearly and without apology:
I want this.

Step 4: Say This Out Loud
"I'm allowed to want what I want.
My truth matters.
It's leading me somewhere honest and good."

Your wanting isn't a flaw.
It's a remembering.
And it's part of your wealth.

Chapter Ten
When Gratitude Becomes a Cage

She had done so much inner work.

She had learned to spot the voice that told her to shrink.
She had started to name her wants again.
She was beginning to believe she was allowed to dream.

But still—when that quiet ache surfaced, the one that whispered
I want more—
something inside her tensed up.

Not because she thought the want was wrong,
but because she believed wanting more *while already having*
meant she wasn't grateful enough.

She had a roof over her head.
Food in the fridge.
People who loved her.
Moments that mattered.

She *knew* she was lucky.
She *was* grateful.

So when she craved more ease, more support, more wealth,
her inner voice scolded her:
"You should be happy with what you have."

She didn't want to be greedy.
Didn't want to seem entitled.
Didn't want to forget how far she'd come.

So she gave gratitude the final say.

She told herself to be content.
She told herself to stop asking.
She told herself to settle.

And that would've been fine—if it felt like truth.
But it didn't.
It felt like a silencing.

Because here's what she eventually saw:
Gratitude that comes with shame is not real gratitude.
It's a performance.
It's a quiet cage disguised as grace.

She was allowed to be grateful *and* want more.

Her longing wasn't from lack.
It was from truth.
It was from the part of her that was waking up—again and again—
to who she really was.

Wanting more wasn't selfish.
It was honest.

She didn't crave more for the sake of appearance or status.
She craved it because her soul was expanding.
Because her body was tired of pretending she didn't want what

she wanted.
Because she was finally safe enough to admit it.

Eventually, the voice inside her softened.
It said:

"You can love your life and still want more ease.
You can be thankful and still long for more support.
You can have enough and still be ready for what's next."

Gratitude and wanting weren't enemies.
They were partners.
One rooted her in presence.
The other called her forward.

She didn't have to choose between them.
She could hold both—fully, freely, and without apology.

Money Wisdom

Wanting more doesn't make you ungrateful.
It makes you honest.
Gratitude says, *this matters to me.*
Longing says, *and so does this.*

You can be deeply thankful for what you've built
and still feel a pull toward something more.
More aligned.
More supportive.
More true.

You weren't meant to stay frozen in one version of enough.
Your needs, values, and visions are allowed to evolve.
That evolution is not a betrayal of gratitude—it's a continuation of it.

Let your appreciation root you.
Let your honest wants move you.
Both are sacred.
And both belong.

Soul Bank Practice: Holding Gratitude and Growth

Step 1: Ground in What's Good
Write down a few things in your life or finances you feel genuinely thankful for.
Not to guilt yourself—but to ground yourself in truth.

Step 2: Name the "More" You Long For
Now write down what your heart is quietly asking for.
Ease? Breathing room? Time? Wealth? Freedom?
Let yourself name it—even if it feels uncomfortable.

Step 3: Notice the Guilt Story
What do you hear when you say you want more?
Do you hear:
"You should be content"?
"That's selfish"?
"Others have it worse"?
Name those stories. Then ask: *Are they true? Or are they just old conditioning?*

Step 4: Say This Out Loud
"I am deeply grateful for what is.
And I am allowed to grow beyond it.
Both can be true.
Both are worthy.
And I am free to honor them both."

Every time you let gratitude and honest wanting live in the same breath,
you're building a money relationship rooted in truth, not fear.
That's the kind of wealth that lasts.

Chapter Eleven
She Let It Be Easy

She didn't grow up with easy.

Her proudest moments were the ones she *earned*
through sweat, effort, long days, and stress.
She had been taught—directly or not—that value came from working hard.
That effort equaled worth.
That if something came easily, it probably didn't count.

So she learned to make things harder than they needed to be.
Not on purpose.
Just out of habit. Out of survival.

She second-guessed herself.
Overanalyzed the simplest decisions.
Held back joy until every box was checked, every task completed, every outcome secured.

Even with money—especially with money—
she assumed ease was suspicious.

If something flowed, she waited for the catch.
If she felt a moment of peace, her nervous system went on high alert.

If someone helped her, she felt awkward—like she needed to apologize or prove she wasn't a burden.
If money came easily, she questioned whether she deserved it.

Not because she didn't want ease.
But because ease felt unfamiliar.

Her body had learned to link struggle with success.
To link stress with safety.
To feel more comfortable bracing than receiving.

She didn't mean to resist the good.
It just didn't feel safe—yet.

But one day, she paused.

Maybe it was after a kind gesture she wanted to deflect.
Maybe it was after a payment came in with surprising flow.
Maybe it was just a quiet morning when everything felt okay.

And she wondered:

What if this could be okay?
What if ease was allowed too?

What if she didn't have to hustle to earn rest?
Didn't have to prove her worth to feel supported?
Didn't have to struggle to be respected?

What if her money journey could feel gentler?

It felt radical, almost rebellious, to consider.
But she was tired of the tightness.
Tired of equating burnout with pride.
Tired of thinking she had to *deserve* ease.

So, little by little, she softened.

She let herself take the aligned path—not just the hard one.
She let herself ask for help without explaining.
She let herself enjoy the abundance when it showed up.

And she realized:
Ease didn't mean she wasn't working.
It meant she was working *with* herself, not against her.

It meant she trusted her enough to believe in flow.
And that... was new.

Money Wisdom

You might've been taught that money has to be hard.

That you're only allowed to have it if you've earned it through effort.
That you need to worry over every cent to prove you're responsible.
That burnout is just part of being "good with money."
That struggle means you're doing it right.

But what if that's not true?

Hard isn't the only way.
Guilt doesn't make you more worthy.
And pain is not a requirement.

Ease isn't cheating.
Sometimes, ease is wisdom.

Letting it be easy doesn't mean you don't care.
It doesn't mean you're lazy.
It means you're aligned.
It means you're finally trusting yourself.

You don't have to prove your worth through struggle.
You don't need to grip tighter just to feel deserving.

You can choose lightness.
You can let yourself breathe.
You can receive without guilt.

You are worthy of ease.
You deserve to feel good.

That's not weakness.
That's wealth.

Soul Bank Practice: Letting It Be Easier

Step 1: Name the Story
What were you taught—directly or indirectly—about effort and money?
Examples:
"Money doesn't grow on trees."
"You have to work hard for every dollar."
"If it comes easy, it won't last."
Write down whatever beliefs still linger in the background.

Step 2: Notice Where You Resist Ease
Think of a recent moment when something flowed—
a payment came through, someone offered help, or something aligned with little effort.
Did you let it feel good?
Or did guilt or suspicion creep in?

Step 3: Try a Lighter Way
Pick one area of your money life today—spending, saving, asking, resting.
What would it look like to make it just a little easier?
Even ten percent?
Let that be enough.

Step 4: Say This Out Loud
"I don't have to struggle to be worthy.
I'm allowed to let it be easier.
And I can still grow.
Ease isn't less.
It's just more aligned."

Chapter Twelve
She Was Allowed to Rest

Letting money feel easier was one thing.
Letting herself rest—without guilt—was another.

She didn't grow up seeing rest as something you just did.
It was a reward.
A thing you earned after being productive, helpful, busy, good.

So for a long time, rest felt like something she had to earn.
After the work was done.
After the inbox was cleared.
After the house was clean.
After the debt was paid.
After everyone else was okay.

Only then could she exhale—maybe.

Even when she rested, she didn't really rest.
Her body was still braced.
Her mind still scanning.
Her nervous system still in motion.

She didn't know how to stop.
Because some part of her believed:
If I slow down, it will all fall apart.

And beneath that:
If I slow down, I'll be less worthy.

Rest felt indulgent.
Lazy.
A threat to the image she had worked so hard to maintain—
The one where she had it all together.
Where she didn't need help.
Where she was fine.

But she wasn't fine.
She was tired.

And eventually, she couldn't outrun that truth.
So, she began to practice stopping.

She paused—even when the list was unfinished.
She lay down in the middle of the day, just because.
She let the dishes sit.
She let herself sit.

She didn't always feel good about it.
Sometimes the guilt crept in.
But she kept doing it anyway.

And in the quiet, something new started to emerge.
Not fear.
Not shame.
But softness.
And then a voice—gentle, but clear:

You are allowed to rest.
Not because you've done enough.
But because you are enough.

Money Wisdom

Rest is not a reward for productivity.
It's a basic human need.

But when money feels tied to worth, rest can feel dangerous.
You might catch yourself thinking you haven't earned it.
That there's too much to do.
That you'll relax later—when things feel more stable, more certain, more "deserving."

But rest isn't a luxury for someday.
It's a resource for today.
It strengthens your nervous system.
It supports your decision-making.
It brings you back into alignment—so your money choices come from clarity, not chaos.

And yes, that includes actually taking your vacation days.
You don't have to hoard them like proof of responsibility.
You don't have to wait until you're burned out to step away.
Use them.
Use them without guilt.
Because rest isn't falling behind—it's remembering who you are when you're not in survival mode.

You don't have to prove your value to pause.
You don't need to hit a number to lay down the weight.
You are allowed to breathe.
To soften.
To stop holding it all.

You don't just deserve rest.
You *need* it.
And that need doesn't make you weak.
It makes you wise.

Soul Bank Practice: Relearning Rest

Step 1: Notice the Pattern
Where do you feel like you have to "earn" rest?
What do you tell yourself you must finish first before it's okay to stop?

Step 2: Question the Story
Whose voice is that?
Where did you learn that slowing down means falling behind?

Step 3: Practice Permission
Pick one thing today that feels restful.
Let yourself do it without finishing your to-do list first.
Even five minutes counts.

Step 4: Say This Out Loud
"I am allowed to rest.
Not because everything is done.
But because I am worthy of ease right now."

Each time you pause on purpose,
you're depositing into your Soul Bank.
And building a version of wealth
that includes your wellbeing.

Chapter Thirteen
She Stopped Comparing

It started with one scroll.
Just a glance.
A house she didn't have.
A vacation she didn't take.
A woman who somehow looked joyful, successful, rested—and rich.
And that bag.

In a single second, her peace slipped away.

She had been feeling okay.
Proud of how far she'd come.
Grateful for what she had.

But now?

Now she felt behind.
Small.
Like she wasn't doing enough.
Like she wasn't enough.

It's wild how fast comparison works.
Her friend's promotion made her question her own path.
Her sister's savings made her debt feel heavier.

Even strangers on the internet suddenly felt like proof that she was failing.

Without realizing it, she started chasing things she didn't even want.
A lifestyle that didn't match her values.
A version of success that didn't fit her soul.
A giant vehicle that didn't make sense for her—but looked right in the photo.

It was like her own compass got hijacked.
She lost track of what mattered to *her*.
Because everyone else's life looked shinier, faster, better.

But eventually, she paused.
And asked a different question:

What actually feels good to me?

Not what looks good.
Not what sounds impressive.
Not what other people think is success.

What feels like peace?

And slowly, she found her way back.
To her own timing.
To her own values.
To her own enoughness.

Because comparison might be loud—
but truth always brings you home.

Money Wisdom

Comparison messes with your clarity.
It turns someone else's life into a measuring stick—
and suddenly, your joy feels too small,
your progress feels too slow,
and your wins don't feel like they count.

But your money path is your own.
So is your timing.
So is your version of enough.

You don't have to keep up.
You don't have to match their pace.
You definitely don't have to spend your energy chasing a life
that was never meant for you.

Money feels better when it's aligned—
not just impressive.
When it reflects *your* real priorities,
not someone else's highlight reel.

You're allowed to want what you want.
You're allowed to define wealth on your terms.
You're allowed to feel proud without needing proof.

There's no gold star for living someone else's dream.
The only version of success that matters
is the one that feels like *you*.

Soul Bank Practice: Reclaiming Your Enough

Step 1: Notice the Comparison Triggers
Who or what tends to knock you off center when it comes to money?
A certain friend? A social media scroll?
Family dinners with subtle bragging?
Name them. Not to blame—but to become aware.
Awareness is how you take your power back.

Step 2: Get Honest About What's Actually Yours
Choose one thing you've been chasing lately—
a number, a lifestyle, a "goal."
Ask yourself:
Do I truly want this?
Or do I just think I should?

Step 3: Redefine Wealth for Yourself
What does real wealth feel like to *you*?
Not what it looks like on Instagram.
But what it feels like in your body, your home, your day-to-day life.
Is it peace? Space? Freedom? Support? Simplicity?

Step 4: Say This Out Loud
"I release the need to compare.
I'm on my own timeline.
I define wealth in a way that feels true to me."

The more you come home to what's real for *you*,
the quieter the noise gets.
Comparison steals presence.
Clarity brings it back.

Chapter Fourteen
She Stopped Rushing

She thought she was behind.
Behind on savings.
Behind on home ownership.
Behind on building wealth, getting stable, having it figured out.

She'd look around and think,
"I should be further along by now."

It didn't matter how far she'd come.
How much she had learned.
How many quiet wins she had created for herself.

The shame of not being *there yet* always seemed louder.

And the world didn't help.
Timelines were everywhere—sometimes obvious, sometimes quiet.
The age you should hit certain milestones.
The pressure to buy the house, land the job, build the wealth… early.
The message that if you didn't start soon enough, you missed your chance.

The constant hum of *you're late.*

So she rushed.
Tried to fix it all overnight.
Pushed herself harder.
Tried to prove she wasn't behind.

She scrambled.
She burned out.
All in the name of *catching up*.

Until one day, her body said, *enough*.
Not with words.
With tension in her chest.
With that wired-but-tired feeling that never let her rest.
With the quiet sense that no matter how much she did—it was never enough.

And something clicked.

Maybe she wasn't behind.
Maybe her timeline wasn't broken.
Maybe she was right on time—for her.

Money Wisdom

We're handed so many stories about what success is supposed to look like—
and when it should happen.

By thirty, you should own a home.
By forty, you should have it all saved.
By fifty, you should be coasting.

But says who?

There's no one right timeline.
No magic age for having it all figured out.
No financial milestone that gets to define your worth.

What really matters is that you're moving from alignment, not panic.
That your decisions feel true, not like a performance.
That your pace is yours—honest, steady, and real.

You're not behind.
You're on *your* path.
And it might look completely different from anyone else's.

That's not a problem.
That's your power.

It's not about how fast you arrive.
It's about who you're becoming along the way.

Soul Bank Practice: Releasing the Rush

Step 1: Name the Pressure
Finish this sentence:
"I feel like I should be further along in..."
Let it be honest. Let it sting if it needs to. This is where the healing starts.

Step 2: Ask Where It Came From
Who gave you that timeline?
Was it your family? School? Social media?
Whose voice told you that you were behind—and is that a voice you still want to listen to?

Step 3: Choose a Kinder Truth
What if you're not behind at all?
What if this is exactly where you're meant to be?
Write down one gentle, grounded version of that truth.

Step 4: Say This Out Loud
"I am not behind.
I am right on time—for me.
I trust the pace of my becoming."

Every time you speak that truth, you loosen the grip of comparison.
You come home to your own rhythm.

There's no medal for rushing.
But there is peace in presence
and power in trusting your unfolding.

Chapter Fifteen
She No Longer Tied Her Worth to the Numbers

For a long time, the numbers told her who she was.

The savings account balance.
The credit card debt.
The income that came in—or didn't.
The price she could charge without flinching.
The raise she was hoping for.
The goal she did—or didn't—hit.

Every number felt personal.
If things were up, she felt like she was doing well.
If they dropped, she spiraled.
She'd question her decisions, her direction, even her value.

She didn't always say it out loud, but deep down, the math felt like a mirror.
Am I smart enough?
Am I responsible enough?
Am I secure enough?
Am I enough?

She wasn't chasing numbers—she was chasing safety.
And trying to outrun the quiet shame that whispered, "You should be further along."

But one day, she paused.
Looked at the numbers.
Felt the familiar wave of emotion rise.
And asked herself something new:

What if these numbers don't define me?
What if I'm still worthy—even here?

It didn't mean she stopped caring.
It meant she stopped confusing net worth with self-worth.
She stopped handing over her value to a number on a screen.
She started rooting into something deeper.
Something steadier.
Something that didn't rise and fall with her bank account.

She didn't ignore the numbers.
She just stopped letting them speak louder than her truth.

Because she was already enough—long before anything was "figured out."
And that truth?
That was the real wealth.

Money Wisdom

You are not your balance sheet.
You are not the number in your bank account.
You are not your debt.
You are not your income.

But in a world that ranks everything—
where more is often seen as better,

where success is measured in digits,
where being "bad with money" feels like a personal flaw—
it's easy to forget that.

The truth is, numbers are just information.
They're neutral—until we give them meaning.
And too often, we make them mean something about who we are.

But your worth isn't up for debate.
It doesn't rise and fall with your paycheck.
It doesn't disappear when you overspend.
It doesn't improve when your balance grows.

You were always worthy.
Even when things felt messy.
Even when you were learning.
Even when the numbers didn't look how you wanted them to.

Your money can change.
Your story can evolve.
But your worth?
That stays.

And the more you root into that truth,
the more your money gets to grow
without having to prove anything.

Soul Bank Practice: Separating Worth from Wealth

Step 1: Catch the Pattern
Think back to a recent moment—
a bill that felt heavy,
a balance that made your chest tighten,
a goal you didn't meet.
Did you make that number mean something about you?
Write down what happened, honestly and without judgment.

Step 2: Call It Out
Now ask yourself:
What did that number make me feel?
Where do I think that feeling came from?
Was there an old belief underneath it—like "I'm not good with money" or "I'm falling behind"?
Name the story.

Step 3: Rewrite the Meaning
Take that same moment,
and this time, respond like you would to a friend.
What's a more compassionate truth you can offer yourself?
Write it down, gently and clearly.

Step 4: Say This Out Loud
"Numbers don't define me.
They might inform my next step—
but they don't get to decide my value.
I am already enough.
I always have been."

Let your money grow.
Let your goals stretch.
Let your numbers change.
But never let them shrink your truth.

You are already rich in the ways that matter most.

Chapter Sixteen
She Learned to Forgive Her Past Self

There were moments she couldn't stop replaying.
The money she spent on those overpriced shoes that weren't even comfortable.
The savings she used up on a trip with her ex.
The things she didn't ask for.
The advice she didn't listen to.
The times she said yes when she really wanted to say no.

She judged herself for all of it.
Quietly.
Harshly.
Even when no one else knew.
Even after she had grown and changed.

She kept punishing her past self
for not doing better.

But the truth was—
she didn't know better then.
She was surviving.
She was figuring it out.
She was making the best decisions she could

with the tools she had at the time.

And eventually, she realized:
growth doesn't mean never messing up.
It means seeing the wisdom in those messy moments—
and recognizing they were never really mistakes to begin with.

The real growth?
Is choosing compassion over shame.
Again and again.

Money Wisdom

Your past self was never your enemy.
She was doing the best she could.
And she's the one who got you here.

Maybe she avoided money.
Maybe she overspent.
Maybe she waited too long, or moved too fast.

You can still honor the lessons—
without carrying the guilt.

Because punishing yourself doesn't create peace.
And shame never built anything worth standing on.

Forgiveness doesn't mean pretending it didn't happen.
It just means you stop making yourself pay for it again.

You're allowed to grow
and still love the version of you who didn't know how.

You can look back with kindness instead of blame.
You can stop trying to be perfect.
You can let yourself be fully, completely human.

And that kind of grace?
That's the wealth that lasts.

Soul Bank Practice: Offering Yourself Grace

Step 1: Name the Memory
What's one money decision you still feel a sting of regret about?
Write it down—honestly, but without judgment.

Step 2: Speak to Her
Picture the version of you who made that choice.
What was she going through?
What did she believe?
What did she need in that moment?
Write her a short, kind note—from the you who knows more now.

Step 3: Rewrite the Loop
Instead of replaying the moment you wish you could change, focus on how you've grown.
What do you understand now that you didn't then?
How are you showing up differently because of it?

Step 4: Say This Out Loud
"I forgive the version of me who didn't know yet.
She was doing her best.
She deserves kindness, not shame."

You don't need to keep apologizing for your past.
You get to keep becoming—
with more wisdom, more softness, and more peace.

Chapter Seventeen
She Saw the Pattern, and This Time She Chose Differently

He knew this feeling.
She had been here before.

Saying yes when she meant maybe.
Lowering her rate because it felt easier than asking for what she was worth.
Overdelivering to feel valuable.
Avoiding the spreadsheet.
Justifying things she didn't actually feel okay about.
Trying to prove she wasn't too much, too needy, too expensive.

She had seen this pattern before.
The shrinking.
The guilt.
The pressure to perform or prove.
And even though she had named it, naming it wasn't the same as changing it.

For a while, the pattern still ran in the background.
Quietly guiding her choices.
Steering her away from her own truth.

But something shifted.
Maybe it was softness.
Maybe it was strength.

Because this time, when the familiar moment came
when she was about to agree to something that didn't feel right
when she almost offered the discount before being asked
when she nearly told herself to just be grateful and move on
she paused.

And in that pause, she remembered.

She didn't have to betray herself to be safe.
She didn't have to make herself smaller to be liked.
She didn't have to choose fear just because it was familiar.

So she chose something else.
Maybe it was subtle.
Maybe no one else noticed.
But it mattered.

She chose to honor her knowing.
To hold her worth.
To speak honestly.
And that choice
that one small, quiet choice
was a turning point.

The pattern didn't get to decide anymore.
She did.

Money Wisdom

Awareness is powerful.
But real change happens in the choosing.

Most of our money patterns are not random.
They come from old conditioning.
From ways we learned to stay safe.
From beliefs we absorbed.
From habits that helped us survive.

You do not shift a pattern by judging yourself for having it.
You shift it by choosing differently.
One moment.
One decision.
One breath at a time.

You might still feel the pull.
To give more than you have.
To stay quiet instead of asking for what is fair.
To accept less than you are worth.
To avoid the conversation.

But that pause
where something in you says
wait, maybe I do not have to do it this way
that is the opening.
That is the shift.

This is where financial freedom begins.
Not just in your bank account
but in your body
your breath
your voice.

Every time you choose from who you are becoming
instead of who you used to be
you change the story.
And every one of those moments matters.

Soul Bank Practice: The Power of One Different Choice

Step 1: Spot the Pattern

What's one money habit or reaction you keep falling into that doesn't feel good anymore?
Something you know isn't helping, but it's been hard to change.
Maybe it's:
- Saying yes when you really want to say no
- Avoiding your bank account
- Undercharging or overgiving
- Feeling guilty when you spend on yourself

Write it down without shame—just honesty.

Step 2: Notice What Sets It Off

What usually triggers that pattern?
Is it stress? Fear? A certain person or situation?
Where do you feel it in your body? What thoughts start spinning?

Step 3: Choose a New Way—Once

What would doing it differently look like, even just one time?
Maybe it's pausing before you say yes.
Maybe it's checking your balance with kindness.
Maybe it's naming your rate without over-explaining.
It doesn't have to be huge. Just a real shift.

Step 4: Say This Out Loud

"I'm allowed to grow beyond this pattern.
I don't have to keep repeating what no longer serves me.
One choice in alignment with who I'm becoming is enough to begin.
This is how things change—one honest moment at a time."

Chapter Eighteen
She Stopped Feeling Ashamed of What She Didn't Know

She used to nod along in financial conversations
even when she had no idea what the terms and jargon meant.

She'd smile politely at the banker,
pretend to understand the fine print,
and make a mental note to Google it later.

Sometimes she did attempt to research it—
only to feel even more confused.

So she'd close the tab.
Push it aside.
Tell herself, I'll figure it out eventually.

But deep down, she felt ashamed.

Like she should already know.
Like she had somehow failed for not learning it earlier.
Like she wasn't smart enough to catch up now.

She Stopped Feeling Ashamed of What She Didn't Know

She didn't want to ask the "dumb" questions.
Didn't want to admit she was unsure.

So she stayed quiet.

But silence didn't bring safety.
It only deepened the shame.

Until one day she realized:
No one is born knowing this.
And the system wasn't built to make it easy.

She wasn't behind.
She wasn't broken.
She just hadn't been taught.

And now—she was willing to learn.

Money Wisdom

There is no shame in not knowing.

Financial systems are often filled with jargon, gatekeeping, and assumptions.

And most of us weren't taught this growing up—especially not women.

So of course you feel unsure.
Of course you second-guess.
Of course you freeze when the language feels too big.

But not knowing doesn't mean you're not capable.
It just means you're human.
And that you're at the beginning of something new.

The most powerful shift you can make?
Replacing shame with curiosity.

Asking the question.
Taking the class.
Sitting in the discomfort and staying open.

You don't have to know everything.
You just have to stay willing.

Your learning is not too late.
It's right on time.

Soul Bank Practice: Releasing Shame, Reclaiming Curiosity

Step 1: Own the Gap Without Judgment
What's one area of money that still feels confusing or overwhelming to you?
Write it down honestly, without sugarcoating or self-blame.

Step 2: Find the Origin
Where did you first absorb the idea that you should already know this?
A school experience? A conversation? A cultural message?

Step 3: Choose One Thing to Learn
Pick one small thing you're curious to understand better.
It could be how a certain type of investment account works
how to ask for a raise
or what investing really means.
Let this be an act of empowerment, not pressure.

Step 4: Say This Out Loud
"I am allowed to not know.
And I am safe to learn.
Shame doesn't serve me—curiosity does."

This isn't about perfection.
It's about presence.
And you're already showing up.

Chapter Nineteen
She Redefined What It Meant to Be "Good with Money"

She thought being good with money meant being good at math.
Or spreadsheets.
Or negotiating.
Or budgeting.
Or investing.
Or knowing exactly what to do, all the time.

She didn't see herself in that version.

She was intuitive.
Emotional.
Creative.
A slow processor.
A deep feeler.

So she labeled herself bad with money and carried the shame like a hidden weight.

But what if that wasn't true?

What if being good with money
didn't mean being perfect with numbers
but being connected to your values?

What if it meant awareness, not control?
Clarity, not constant calculation?

What if being good with money
looked like feeling safe in your decisions?
Staying in relationship with your finances, even when it's uncomfortable?
Choosing from alignment, not fear?

She was already good with money.
She just didn't know it yet.

Money Wisdom

We've been taught a narrow definition of financial success often one rooted in hustle, precision, performance, and pressure.

But that's not the only way.

Being good with money can mean:

- Knowing when to spend on joy
- Trusting your timing
- Healing your nervous system around finances
- Feeling safe asking for what you deserve
- Staying curious, even when you're still learning
- Making decisions that honor both your future and your peace

Being good with money isn't about having it all figured out. It's about staying in relationship with it—without shame or avoidance.

It's emotional.
It's relational.
It's alive.

And yes, it's allowed to feel deeply human.

Soul Bank Practice: Defining It on Your Terms

Step 1: Rewrite the Script

What beliefs have you carried about what it means to be good with money?
Examples:
I have to stick to a strict budget
I should already know how to invest
If I have debt, I'm doing it wrong

Step 2: Get Honest About What Actually Feels Good

Think of a moment when you made a money decision that felt aligned
even if it didn't look perfect on paper.
What felt good about it?

Step 3: Write Your Own Definition

Complete this sentence:
Being good with money, for me, means...
Let your truth come through—not the old shoulds.

Step 4: Say This Out Loud

"I don't have to fit someone else's version of success.
I can define financial well-being in a way that reflects who I really am.
And I'm already doing better than I thought."

There's no one right way to be with money.
There's only your way—rooted in truth, clarity, and care.

Chapter Twenty
She Realized She Wasn't Starting From Scratch

It felt like starting over.
Like she was late to the conversation.
Like everyone else had learned something she missed.
Like she had to build her foundation from nothing.

That thought made her feel small.
Tired.
Overwhelmed.
Afraid to even begin.

But slowly, she began to see the truth.

She wasn't starting from scratch.
She was starting from wisdom.
From lived experience.
From lessons that weren't always gentle
but had shaped her deeply.

She wasn't empty.
She was rich with insight.

Yes, there were gaps in knowledge.
Yes, there were things she wished she'd done differently.

But she also knew things—soul things.

How to trust her gut.
How to create beauty from little.
How to stretch a dollar.
How to hold big feelings.
How to keep going.

And all of that mattered.

Money Wisdom

You are not behind.
And you are not blank.
You are not too late.
You are not too far gone.

You are a woman who has lived.
Who has tried.
Who has navigated hard things.
Who has kept showing up, even when it was unclear.

And all of that is wealth.

You don't need to shame your starting point.
You get to honor it.

Because your starting point is not the same as a beginner's.

It's wiser.
It's fuller.
It's ready.

You're not starting from scratch.
You're starting from you.
And that is enough.

Soul Bank Practice: Honoring Where You Begin

Step 1: Name the False Belief
What story have you told yourself about being behind or starting over?
Write it down honestly.

Step 2: Reclaim the Wisdom
Make a list of five things your money journey has already taught you.
Even if they're not technical, they matter.

Step 3: Anchor Into the Truth
Complete this sentence:
I'm not starting from scratch. I'm starting from...
(use your word: experience, growth, clarity, wisdom, love, etc.)

Step 4: Say This Out Loud
"I don't need to start over.
I get to start forward.
I carry wisdom that matters—and I trust where I'm headed."

This isn't a reset.
It's a reclamation.

Chapter Twenty-One
She Became the Source

She used to look outside herself for answers.
For stability.
For permission.
For someone to rescue her from the stress.

She looked to the numbers.
The budgets.
The paychecks.
The experts.
The relationship.
The dream job.
The "someday."

Always something out there
to finally make her feel safe in here.

But the more she healed,
the more she saw the truth:
The source she was seeking was her.

It wasn't a dramatic moment.
It was subtle.
Like waking up and realizing
she no longer needed to prove herself.

She no longer had to wait to be chosen.
She no longer had to earn her way into peace.

She was her own money hero.
The one who could make a plan.
Ask the question.
Track the numbers.
Rewrite the story.
Build the safety she used to think had to come from someone else.

She didn't need a sugar daddy.
She needed to believe in her own worth.

And she did.

Money Wisdom

Many of us were taught—directly or quietly—
to wait for someone else to bring financial security.
To partner our way into stability.
To outsource our worth to someone who "knew better."
To follow the rules, be good, and stay small.

But no more.

Becoming the source means
you stop waiting for outside permission.
You stop outsourcing your intuition.
You stop needing your money journey to look like anyone else's.

You listen to yourself.
You trust your rhythm.
You build a foundation that reflects who you really are.

You don't need to have it all figured out.
You just need to remember your power.

You are the source.
And you always have been.

Soul Bank Practice: Reclaiming Your Inner Source

Step 1: Name What You've Outsourced
Where have you been waiting for someone else to save you financially?
Be honest—not ashamed.

Step 2: Reframe the Story
What if you already have what you need to take the next step?
What does that feel like?

Step 3: Anchor into Agency
Write down one money action you've taken recently that made you feel powerful—
even if it was small.

Step 4: Say This Out Loud
"I am not waiting to be rescued.
I am the source of my safety.
I trust myself to lead—with clarity, strength, and soul."

This is not about doing it all alone.
It's about no longer abandoning yourself.

Chapter Twenty-Two
She Didn't Have to Hustle to Be Worthy

She used to wear her busyness like a badge.
If she was overwhelmed, she felt useful.
If she was exhausted, she felt productive.
If she was hustling, she felt like she was doing it right.

It wasn't just about the money.
It was about being good.
Being enough.
Being seen as valuable.

She worked long hours. Said yes when she meant no.
Overdelivered. Undercharged.
Tried to stay one step ahead of disappointment.
And deep down, she hoped all the doing would finally make her feel safe.
That if she just proved herself enough, the anxiety would quiet.

But it didn't.
The more she hustled, the more she felt like she had to keep earning her place.

The more she gave, the more depleted she became.
And still, the goalposts kept moving.

She thought burnout was just part of the deal.
But eventually—she got tired of being tired.
She didn't want to keep proving her worth through pain.
She didn't want her life to feel like a race she could never win.

So she started asking new questions:
What if rest didn't need to be earned?
What if slowing down wasn't failure?
What if her worth had nothing to do with output?

And what if her money could grow from peace, not just pressure?

That shift didn't happen all at once.
But the moment she stopped tying her value to how much she could do,
everything started to feel a little more free.
And so did she.

Money Wisdom

You've probably been praised for pushing through.
For staying late.
For doing more than was asked.
For sacrificing your time, health, and joy in the name of success.

But that's not wealth.
That's a wound.

Being "good with money" shouldn't mean abandoning yourself.
Financial stability isn't supposed to cost you your peace.
You don't have to hustle to prove your worth.

You are allowed to rest.
You are allowed to receive.
You are allowed to build something that feels like *life*—not just survival.

Let your money support your well-being, not replace it.
Let your work reflect your gifts, not try to justify your existence.

You were already enough.
You still are.
You don't need to earn what you've always had within you.

Soul Bank Practice: Letting Go of Proving

Step 1: Name the Pattern
Where have you been trying to prove your worth through effort or overdoing?
Is it in your job? Your business? How you handle money at home?
What have you felt like you *had* to do in order to feel valuable?

Step 2: Be Honest About the Cost
What has all that proving taken from you?
Time with people you love?
Moments of rest?
Your health? Your joy?

Step 3: Imagine a New Way
What would it look like to work or manage money from a place of enoughness—not pressure?
If you didn't have to *earn* your worth, how would you move through your days?

Step 4: Say This Out Loud
"I don't have to hustle to be worthy.
My rest matters.
My presence is enough.
I am valuable even when I'm still."

Let your money life reflect your worth—not your burnout.

Chapter Twenty-Three
She Didn't Wait to Feel Ready

She thought she had to wait until she felt confident.
Until she knew all the steps.
Until she had more money saved.
Until the debt was gone.
Until the fear disappeared.

She thought readiness would feel calm and clear.
Like a green light from the universe.
Like a sign that said,
Now you're allowed.

But that moment never really came.

Instead, it showed up as a small nudge.
A tiny flicker of knowing.
A quiet whisper that said,
You don't have to be fearless to begin.

So she did the thing.

She opened the account.
She made the phone call.
She asked the question.
She took the step.

Still unsure.

Still shaky.
Still not totally confident.

But not stuck.

And that changed everything.

Because she realized something most people never tell you:
Readiness doesn't come before the leap.
It arrives after.
In the doing.
In the showing up.
In the small moments where you move forward anyway.

She was more ready than she knew.

Money Wisdom

There's a myth that says you have to feel completely confident before you start.
But the truth is—readiness often shows up after the first step, not before.

You don't have to have it all figured out.
You don't need to feel fearless.
You don't need a perfect plan.

You just need to be willing.

Willing to begin.
Willing to learn as you go.
Willing to take one small step with your money—even if you feel unsteady.

Financial empowerment isn't about getting it perfect.
It's about staying present.
Being honest with yourself.
And choosing courage—one decision at a time.

That is more than enough.

Soul Bank Practice: Start Before You Feel Ready

Step 1: Find the Waiting Spot
What's one money-related action you've been putting off until you "feel ready"?
Name it honestly—no shame.

Step 2: Ask What You're Waiting For
More knowledge? More confidence? Less fear?
What do you think needs to happen before you can begin?
Get curious about your version of "ready."

Step 3: Take a Micro Step
What's one small, doable version of that action you could take today?
It doesn't need to be a big leap—just something that breaks the pause.

Step 4: Say This Out Loud
"I don't have to feel fully ready to begin.
Courage meets me in motion.
And every step forward counts."

You're already more ready than you think.
The path will meet you as you walk it.

Chapter Twenty-Four
She Faced the Numbers—And Didn't Fall Apart

She used to avoid them.
The credit card statements.
The bank balance.
The subscriptions she meant to cancel.
The investment accounts she never opened.

Looking at the numbers felt… heavy.
Too real.
Too much.

What if they told her she was failing?
What if they confirmed her fears?
What if she couldn't fix it?

So she avoided.
Pretended not to care.
Made vague guesses instead of clear choices.

But the unknown didn't make her feel safer.
It made her anxious.

Foggy.
Disconnected.

Eventually, she got tired of shrinking from her own life.
Tired of not knowing.

So she looked.

Not all at once.
Not perfectly.
But honestly.

And she didn't fall apart.

She got stronger.

Not because the numbers were perfect—
but because she was finally in relationship with them.

Money Wisdom

Avoidance feels safe—until it isn't.

Not looking at the numbers can feel like protection.
But it often fuels more fear than clarity.

Because it's not the numbers themselves that hurt—
it's the stories we attach to them.

Facing your finances doesn't mean judging them.
It means meeting them with honesty and care.

You get to look with compassion.
With curiosity.
With the energy of *I want to know—so I can grow.*

Financial peace doesn't come from pretending.
It comes from presence.
And presence is power.

Soul Bank Practice: Looking With Love

Step 1: Choose One Area to Face
Pick just one number or category you've been avoiding—
a credit card balance, monthly spending, a bank statement, a tax task.

Step 2: Ground First
Before looking, take three deep breaths.
Say to yourself: I am safe to see this. This is just information. This does not define me.

Step 3: Look—With Curiosity, Not Criticism
Open the app. Read the statement. Do the math.
Then ask: What is this showing me? What's one small step I can take from here?

Step 4: Say This Out Loud
"I am strong enough to face the truth.
My numbers don't scare me anymore.
Knowledge is power—and I'm reclaiming mine."

Looking doesn't make you weak.
It makes you wise.

Chapter Twenty-Five
She Asked for What She Needed—Even When Her Voice Shook

She used to rehearse the conversation
a hundred times in her head.

The raise.
The rate.
The boundary.
The overdue payment.
The price increase.

She'd map it out.
Build the case.
Wait for the perfect time.

Then freeze.

Not because she didn't know what to say—
but because she didn't want to be too much.
Too direct.
Too needy.
Too greedy.

So she kept shrinking.
Swallowing the words.
Absorbing the discomfort.

Telling herself,
It's fine. I'll figure it out. I don't want to cause trouble.

But eventually—
the cost of staying quiet became too high.

So she spoke.

Even with the tremble in her voice.
Even with her heart pounding.

And when she didn't apologize for needing what she needed—
something shifted.

She didn't just say the words.
She stood inside them.

Money Wisdom

There is nothing wrong with asking.
Nothing shameful about needing.
Nothing greedy about valuing yourself.

You're taught to be polite.
To stay agreeable.
To accept what's given.
To wait to be offered instead of asking outright.

But empowerment often begins the moment you say:
Actually, this doesn't work for me.

Asking doesn't make you difficult.
It makes you clear.

And clarity is a gift—
to yourself and to others.

Even if your voice shakes.
Even if your palms sweat.
Even if it takes everything in you to speak—

You're allowed to ask.
To need.
To take up space.
To advocate for your future self.

And you're allowed to do it imperfectly—
with truth,
with heart,
with strength that doesn't need to shout.

Soul Bank Practice: Using Your Voice

Step 1: Choose a Place to Speak Up
What's one money-related conversation you've been avoiding or shrinking in?
A rate increase? Asking for payment? Setting a boundary?

Step 2: Script It Gently
Write out what you wish you could say—just for yourself.
Let it be honest. Clear. Compassionate.

Step 3: Find Your Anchor
What truth or value are you standing for in this ask?
(Example: *I deserve to be paid. I value clarity. I honor my time.*)

Step 4: Say This Out Loud
"I'm allowed to speak up.
Even if it's messy.
Even if I tremble.
My needs are valid.
And I trust myself to voice them."

You don't have to wait to feel fearless.
You just have to be willing to show up with your truth.

Chapter Twenty-Six
She Released the Pressure to Always Be Doing More

There was a time when stillness made her anxious.

If she wasn't actively working on something—
earning, improving, calculating, optimizing—
she felt behind.

She measured progress by movement.
Felt guilty for rest.
Tied her value to how much she was producing.

And even in her healing,
she turned growth into another to-do list.

But eventually, something softened.

She realized she could still be growing,
even in the pause.
She could still be worthy,
even without performing.

She could still be aligned,
even without fixing.

It didn't have to be a sprint.

It could be a rhythm.
One that made space for breath.
One that trusted in timing.
One that honored *enough*.

Money Wisdom

You are allowed to slow down.
To rest.
To integrate.

You don't have to constantly be learning, doing, or improving to be on the right track.

Sustainable wealth—like sustainable anything—requires rhythm.
It requires seasons.

There will be times of deep focus.
Times of maintenance.
Times of stillness.

All of them matter.

Your value doesn't rise and fall with your output.
You are not a machine.
You are a woman in conscious relationship with your money.

And relationships are alive.

You don't have to push to prove.
You don't have to do more to be more.

You are allowed to just be.

Soul Bank Practice: Loosening the Grip

Step 1: Identify the Pressure Point
Where in your money life are you holding yourself to unrealistic standards?
Is it your savings rate? Your timeline? A course you haven't finished?

Step 2: Reframe the Story
What do you believe will happen if you pause or soften?
Now ask: *Is that really true?*

Step 3: Choose a Gentle Next Step
What's one way you can tend to your finances without force?
Example: Check in softly instead of trying to overhaul everything.

Step 4: Say This Out Loud
"I am not behind.
I don't need to rush.
My growth includes pauses—
and I trust the rhythm of my journey."

You are allowed to release the pressure.
And still arrive.

Chapter Twenty-Seven
She Trusted Her Inner Yes-Even If It Didn't Make Sense on Paper

There were moments her brain said, *Be practical.*

But her body whispered, *this is right.*

Times when the numbers didn't line up
the way a spreadsheet would approve—
but something deeper did.

She'd been taught to second-guess that knowing.
To justify it.
To explain it.
To back it up with logic and math.

But intuition doesn't always speak the language of calculators.
It speaks in chills.
In stillness.
In that soft feeling of *this.*

Even if no one else understands.

And when she started listening to that feeling—
not recklessly, but reverently—
everything shifted.

Because it wasn't about impulse.
It was about alignment.

And alignment was always worth honoring.

Money Wisdom

There's a quiet knowing inside you.
It might not show up in numbers or charts.
It might not make perfect sense to anyone else.
But it's real—and it's wise.

You've been taught to explain every choice.
To defend your instincts.
To double-check your gut against something external.

But your body carries its own intelligence.
Your inner yes is not reckless.
It's not irresponsible.
It's your truth—before the world told you to second-guess it.

Sometimes, what aligns won't add up on paper.
But if it adds up in your soul,
that matters too.

Your money journey isn't just about logic.
It's about trust.
And sometimes the best decisions
are the ones that feel right,
even if they look uncertain.

Soul Bank Practice: Listening to Your Inner Yes

Step 1: Recall a Moment of Knowing
Think of a time when something just *felt* right.
Even if the numbers didn't support it.
What did that "yes" feel like in your body?

Step 2: Revisit a Current Decision
Is there a money-related decision in front of you right now
that feels hard to justify—but intuitively right?
Write about it without trying to make it logical.

Step 3: Ask What Alignment Feels Like
What are the physical or emotional cues
you experience when something is aligned?
Make a list you can return to when doubt creeps in.

Step 4: Say This Out Loud
"I trust my knowing.
Even if it doesn't make perfect sense.
Even if no one else understands.
My intuition is wise.
My alignment matters."

Chapter Twenty-Eight
She Stopped Chasing More Just to Feel Enough

There was a time when *more* felt like the answer.
More money.
More clients.
More security.
More proof.

She thought if she could just earn more,
save more,
build more—
she'd finally feel safe.
Finally feel proud.
Finally feel like she'd made it.

But *more* kept moving the finish line.
No number ever fully filled the gap.

So she got curious.
What was she really trying to earn?
Peace?
Freedom?
Permission to rest?

She began to notice where *more* had become a mask,
not a goal.
A way to feel enough,
instead of remembering she already was.

And she stopped chasing.
Not because she stopped growing,
but because she started choosing growth that meant something.

Growth that was rooted.
Aligned.
Whole.

She realized:
Enough isn't out there.
It's something you decide to feel.

Money Wisdom

There's nothing wrong with wanting more.
More income.
More ease.
More support.

But when *more* becomes the requirement to feel worthy,
it stops being wealth.
It becomes a trap.

You don't have to earn your way into peace.
You can choose peace *while* you grow—
not just after.

The world will always offer one more thing to fix.
One more metric to chase.
One more upgrade to reach.

But you get to pause and ask:
Is this what I truly want?
Or just what I think I'm supposed to want?

Want what you want—boldly.
But let it come from truth, not fear.
From wholeness, not lack.

Soul Bank Practice: Choosing Enough

Step 1: Define Enough for Yourself
If you weren't chasing someone else's version of success, what would *enough* look and feel like to you?

Step 2: Notice the Hidden More
Where are you still believing you have to do, earn, or achieve more just to feel okay?

Step 3: Anchor to What Matters
What do you already have that reflects the life you're building? Gratitude is a powerful antidote to performative *more*.

Step 4: Say This Out Loud
"I don't need more to prove my worth.
I can want from wholeness, not from emptiness.
I am allowed to feel enough—right now."

More is not the enemy.
But it doesn't get to define your value.

Chapter Twenty-Nine
She Realized It Wasn't Just About the Money-It Was About Her Freedom

At first, it was about survival.
Paying the bills.
Catching up.
Digging out.

Then it became about stability.
Saving.
Planning.
Knowing she could handle what came next.

But underneath it all,
it was always about freedom.

The freedom to say no.
To say yes.
To walk away.
To rest.
To choose what was right for her.

Money was never just about dollars.
It was about options.

About agency.
About not staying small because she had no other choice.

And when she began to see it that way,
money stopped being just a stressor or a symbol.
It became a tool.
A companion.
A way of honoring her life.

Money Wisdom

Money is never the end goal.
It's the means.
The mirror.
The amplifier.

It reflects what you believe is possible
and what you feel safe enough to claim.

For so many women,
money has been wrapped up in silence.
In sacrifice.
In staying small.

So healing your relationship with money
isn't just about building wealth—
it's about reclaiming your voice.
Your power.
Your choices.

You're allowed to want financial freedom.
Not to escape your life,
but to fully live it.

To make decisions from clarity, not fear.
To walk into rooms without shrinking.
To create a life that reflects who you really are.

Soul Bank Practice: Defining Freedom

Step 1: Ask What Freedom Means to You
When you imagine true financial freedom,
what does it actually look and feel like in your life?
Be honest. Be specific. Let it be yours—not someone else's version.

Step 2: Notice Where You Already Have It
Where do you already experience even small pockets of choice, space, or ease?
Name them.
Honor them.
Freedom often starts in quiet moments.

Step 3: Identify the Next Layer
Where does money still feel like a leash instead of a key?
Is it a specific bill, situation, or pattern?
What would it take—emotionally, practically, or energetically—to loosen it?

Step 4: Say This Out Loud
"I am allowed to be free.
Money can support—not control—my choices.
This journey isn't just about wealth.
It's about wholeness.
I'm not just building a richer life.
I'm building a freer one."

Chapter Thirty
A Life That Holds All of You

She doesn't need to have it all figured out.
She's not chasing the next financial milestone to feel safe.
Not proving her worth through productivity.
Not trying to be the one who never messes up.

She's building differently now.
From clarity.
From intention.
From the part of her that trusts
not because everything is certain,
but because she is.

She still has questions.
She still double-checks the numbers.
She still forgets and remembers again.

But she no longer abandons herself in the process.
She no longer confuses chaos for aliveness.
She no longer treats burnout as a badge of honor.
She no longer performs safety
she builds it, for real.

And what she builds now
isn't just wealth.

It's sovereignty.
It's spaciousness.
It's a life that holds her.

Because she's no longer building from lack.
She's building from remembrance.
From enoughness.
From love.
From soul.

Money Wisdom

There's no perfect ending to this story.
No flawless spreadsheet.
No magic number that will complete you.

But there is a path.
A path back to you.
A path that honors your truth, your values, your voice.

A path that includes mistakes and pauses and pivots—
and still leads forward.

You don't have to build fast.
You don't have to build like anyone else.
You just have to build from wholeness.

Let your wealth reflect who you really are.
Let your life reflect what matters most.

And know that whatever comes next,
you are ready.
Not because it's easy.
But because it's yours.

Soul Bank Practice: A New Foundation

Step 1: Reflect on Your Journey
What are three truths you've remembered about yourself through this process?
Let them rise—honest, clear, and real.

Step 2: Define What You're Building Now
What does soul rich living mean to you in this season of your life?
Less about numbers. More about values, energy, and ease.

Step 3: Choose Your Anchor Phrase
Pick one sentence to hold onto when things feel shaky.
Let it root you. Let it remind you.
Examples:
"I trust myself with money."
"My worth is not up for debate."
"I build slow, real, and free."

Step 4: Say This Out Loud
"This isn't the end.
It's the foundation.
And I'm building something that honors all of me."

Acknowledgments

To every woman who has ever questioned her worth, her enoughness, or her value—this book is for you.

To the mentors, money teachers, soul guides, and quiet conversations that helped me rewrite my own money story, thank you for helping me come home.

And to every reader walking this path in her own way:
Your healing matters.
Your peace is generational.
And your story is far from over.

www.ingramcontent.com/pod-product-compliance
Lightning Source LLC
Chambersburg PA
CBHW050329010526
44119CB00050B/728